READERS FOR TEENS

The Birthday Present

Luiz H. Rose
Maiza Fatureto
Tereza Sekiya

Series coordinator
Sérgio Varela

CAMBRIDGE
UNIVERSITY PRESS

University Printing House, Cambridge CB2 8BS, United Kingdom

One Liberty Plaza, 20th Floor, New York, NY 10006, USA

477 Williamstown Road, Port Melbourne, VIC 3207, Australia

4843/24, 2nd Floor, Ansari Road, Daryaganj, Delhi – 110002, India

79 Anson Road, #06-04/06, Singapore 079906

Cambridge University Press is part of the University of Cambridge.
It furthers the University's mission by disseminating knowledge in the pursuit of
education, learning and research at the highest international levels of excellence.

http://cambridge.org/elt/readersforteens/

© Cambridge University Press 2008

This publication is in copyright. Subject to statutory exception
and to the provisions of relevant collective licensing agreements,
no reproduction of any part may take place without the written
permission of Cambridge University Press.

First published 2008
20 19 18 17 16 15 14 13 12 11 10 9 8 7 6 5

Printed in Mexico by Editorial Impresora Apolo, S.A. de C.V.

ISBN 978-0-521-04845-3 paperback

Cambridge University Press has no responsibility for the persistence or accuracy
of URLs for external or third-party internet websites referred to in this publication,
and does not guarantee that any content on such websites is, or will remain, accurate
or appropriate.

Illustrations by Alcy Linares

Art direction, book design and layout services: A+ Comunicação, Brazil

Contents

Chapter 1
The money 5

Chapter 2
At the mall 8

Chapter 3
Where's the present? 12

Chapter 4
The idea 14

Chapter 5
The birthday party 18

Chapter 1
The money

Alice studies at Kent International School. She's a good student and she loves art. She can draw great pictures.

Alice has a lot of friends, but Ellen is her best friend. Alice and Ellen do many things together.

One day, Alice tells her mother that Ellen's birthday is on September 15. It's next Sunday.

Alice shows her mother the invitation to Ellen's party.

"Ellen is a nice girl," says Alice's mother. "Let's see. Where's my bag?"

"It's on the chair in the kitchen," answers Alice.

"Oh, thanks," says Alice's mother. "Here's some money. Buy a nice present for Ellen."

"Great!" says Alice. "Thanks a lot, Mom!"

"Be careful with the money!" says her mother.

"OK, mom!" says Alice.

Chapter 2
At the mall

Ellen's birthday party is soon, so Alice goes to the mall to buy Ellen's gift.

There are a lot of nice stores in the mall. Alice sees a candy store. She loves candy. Alice goes into the store and she buys some candy. She eats it all. It's delicious.

Then Alice sees a music store. She loves rock music and she sees a CD by her favorite singer, King. She's so excited! She buys the CD.

There is also a big bookstore in the mall. Alice sees many magazines with photographs of her favorite movie stars. She buys three magazines.

Alice looks at her watch.

"Gee, it's late!" she thinks.

She goes to a department store. She sees a nice blouse for Ellen. But there's a problem. She has no more money for Ellen's present.

Chapter 3
Where's the present?

It's 7:00 o'clock, now, and Alice is at home. She has a new rock CD and three new magazines.

"Hi, Alice! You're late. Let's have dinner!" Alice's mother says.

During dinner her mother asks, "Where's the present for Ellen?"

"Well, I…hmm…I have these magazines," says Alice.

"That isn't a present, Alice!" says her mother. "Where's the money?"

"There's no more money. I have these magazines and this new CD. It's my favorite rock singer," says Alice.

"Oh, Alice! It's important to be careful with money."

"Please, Mom. Give me more money for the present," Alice says.

"Sorry, Alice. I have no more money for you," her mother answers.

Chapter 4
The idea

It's Saturday night. Tina, one of Alice's friends, is at her house.

"What's wrong Alice? Are you sad?" Tina asks.

"Yes, I am. I'm really sad. I have no money. I have no present for Ellen," Alice says. "I don't want to go to Ellen's party."

"Give her your new CD," Tina suggests.

"No, Ellen doesn't like that singer," Alice says.

"Come on, Alice. Ellen is your friend, right?" Tina says.

"Yeah, but..."

"Wait! I have an idea. Let me see some of your pictures," Tina says.

Alice shows her pictures to Tina.

"These are great! Give one to Ellen for her birthday," says Tina.

"Good idea! I can make her a nice card, too," adds Alice.

"Yes, and I can help you with the card," says Tina.

The girls finish the special card in an hour.
"Wow, this is really cool!" Alice says.

Chapter 5
The birthday party

It's now Sunday evening. Alice and Tina go to Ellen's house for Ellen's birthday party. Alice has her present for Ellen, and Tina has a present for Ellen, too.

There are a lot of people at the party. There's music, food, and drinks, too. It's really exciting.

"Hi, Alice and Tina! How are you?" asks Ellen.

"Hi, Ellen," the girls say. "Happy birthday!"

"Thanks!" Ellen says.

"Here's your present, Ellen," Tina says.

"Thank you, Tina," Ellen says. She opens the present. It's a T-shirt.

"It's really nice. I love it," Ellen says.

"Well, I have a little surprise, too" Alice says.

"What is it?" Ellen asks.

"It's just a little thing," Alice says. She gives Ellen the card and the picture.

Ellen reads the card and looks at the picture.

"Wow, this picture is great! And so is the card. You're a great artist, Alice. You can really draw. Thank you," says Ellen.

"Presents are nice, but you know what is more important?" Ellen asks.

"No, what is it?" Alice and Tina ask.

"It is important that you are here tonight. My friends are my birthday present. You are all very special to me," Ellen answers.

The girls smile and hug each other. "Come on now, let's dance!" Ellen adds.